Praise for

"*Not from God* is written in an authentic and inspiring way to help other sojourners come out from darkness and into the light of God's mercy and grace."

> Jessica Honegger, founder and co-CEO of Noonday Collection, author of *Imperfect Courage*, and host of the *Going Scared* podcast

"This beautiful little book you're holding will be your guide to remembering truth, replacing lies, and reflecting on who God is in your daily life. Kaitlin examines ten common thoughts we all have, reveals how they are absolutely not from God, and gives us the truth. She is down to earth, charming, and full of life!"

> Amy Seiffert, author of *Chin Up: Wearing Grace, Strength, and Dignity when Motherhood Unravels Our Souls*

"I've heard it said that the gospel of John is deep enough for an elephant to swim, but shallow enough for children to wade. In *Not From God*, Kaitlin employs a similar style of making wise things simple. She so clearly defines ten strategies of satan that mere babes in Christ can taste and see God's goodness, while older Christians have the chance to discover fresh insight on which to chew. What a wonderful small group resource to blend the generations!"

> Donna Jackson, author of *Temple Sweepers, Everyday Heroes, and Freedom for the Good Little Church Girl*

"Kaitlin Chappell Rogers is a millennial with wisdom beyond her years. The depth of her personal relationship with Jesus echoes in every public word she writes. The way she communicates is clever, concise, conversational, compassionate, and Christ-centered. *Not from God* is a beautiful reminder of everything that is good about Him. This small but rich love offering will leave you encouraged in a big way. From the first sentence to the last, Kaitlin offers up her heart while holding yours every step of the way. No doubt *Not from God* came straight from Him and Kaitlin got the blessing of simply being the conduit of this creative, comforting treasure!"

Katie Wilson, writer, speaker, and painter

"Kaitin's words make life's nonsense make sense. *Not from God* is a counseling session, coffee date with a friend, and a place to connect with God all rolled into one quick read that will help you 'get your life' and embrace the abundant life God promises us in His word."

Toya Poplar, author of *Stop Write There*

Not from God

Taking Back the Narrative of Your Life

kaitlin chappell rogers

Mizpah Publishing House

Not From God
Copyright © 2018 by Kaitlin Chappell Rogers

ISBN: 9781790546060

Cover design by Leslie Knight
Interior artwork by Leslie Knight
Book layout and design by Elizabeth Griffith

This book was written in the nooks and crannies of my life, in between a full time job and learning how to be a new wife. This is my first book and I hope you will treat it with love and kindness. Please forgive me for any mistakes and just look at them as little quirks if you find any. More than anything, I hope this book sparks something in you that makes you want to dig deeper into God's word and see for yourself all the things available from Him.

Published in the United States by Mizpah Card Company with CreateSpace.

First printing September 2018 / Printed in the United States of America

For Caleb,

Thank you for reminding me of all the things that are not from God and that my dreams are always from Him.

Contents

Don't forget that in any darkness you face, the God of light is with you.

Introduction

Take it Back

We have started accepting a narrative for our lives that the world writes for us. We accept emotions and feelings that were never meant for us. We believe lies just because they are spoken over us. That narrative, those feelings, all the lies – they are not from God. Feelings of anxiety and depression and insecurity don't come from our Father. Those things are meant to weigh us down and keep us from feeling light enough to run our race and walk in our purpose.

Peace, contentment, and strength – all of those things do come from God. You simply have to go to Him, drop the heavy load, and pick up the light weights you were meant to carry. John 10:10 says, "The thief comes only to steal and kill and destroy. I came that they may have life and have it abundantly." If we allow the enemy to take over our hearts and minds, he will steal all the joy we have. But, if we decide to put on what Jesus gives us, we will have abundant lives.

With this book and God's Word, you'll begin rewriting the narrative of your life and remembering what is from God and what is not. You are His warrior, and He wants you strong and ready to fight. Learn how to combat everything the enemy throws at you, and do it with grace as you apply these truths to your life.

Are you ready?

Let's give our stories back to God so He can write them the way they were meant to be written. We know how the story ends, but we deserve a really good middle, don't you think?

Anxiety

Philippians 4:6
"Do not be anxious about anything, but in everything by prayer and supplication with thanksgiving let your requests be made known to God."

What do they really think about me? What does my future hold? What if something bad happens to my family? Where will my career take me? What if I never reach my goals and dreams?

These thoughts can swirl around in our heads, make our chests tight, and steal precious time from our days. Anxiety is a major scheme of the enemy to kill and destroy any joy we might have. He wants us focusing on the "what ifs" and the worst-case scenarios so we won't see the goodness of God in front of us.

Since anxiety is from the enemy and not from God, God has power over it, and He dwells within us. Therefore, we have power over it, too. We have the ability to take our thoughts captive, speak truth over the lies, and take back the narrative of what our lives will look like.

Do you leave meetings, encounters, or events and think about every little thing you said? Do you replay things you say or do until you make yourself sick? Do you create the worst possible outcomes in your mind? Anxiety can make us over-analyze every single move we make and take us to really dark places. God tells us not to be anxious about *anything*.

Senior pastor of Elevation Church, Steven Furtick, said, "Not being anxious is not a command – it's a result." When we humble ourselves before God, when we bring everything to Him with prayer, petition, and thanksgiving, the anxiety fades.

You see, we have been gifted constant communication with the Creator of the universe. All we have to do is call on Him to send our anxious thoughts running for the hills. And the enemy won't make it easy. Nope. He will be there hiding and waiting, ready to pounce at our moments of weakness. He's waiting when we start to think of all the reasons why we just don't measure up at school or home or work. He's hiding out, ready to interrupt as soon as we think we might get some sleep instead of running through to-do lists at midnight.

The enemy is clever, not creative. He can't figure out how to come up with new tactics, so he just keeps using old ones with a new coat of paint. Our God is creative. He comes up with new ways to pull us through the moments of weakness. He gives us new outlets to escape the anxiety. He shows us verses we've seen millions of times in a brand new light.

I dwell on things a lot. I always joke my epitaph will say, "She dwelled from 1992 to XXXX" because I can dwell on moments or mistakes or misunderstandings for days and weeks… maybe years. I'll be in the middle of a good mood and satan will drag up something that happened when I was 12 for me to overthink like only I can. Anybody with me? It's his strategy to take my mind off the blessings in front of me so I'll stop praising God and start doubting Him.

But I know prayer, petition, and thanksgiving allow me to dwell on His faithfulness. I know when I go back through my prayer journal and read all the answered prayers, I start to dwell on all He has done. Those mess-ups begin to hold less weight, and His mercy begins to hold more.

"We destroy arguments and every lofty opinion raised against the knowledge of God, and take every thought captive to obey Christ." 2 Corinthians 10:5

The only way to stop overthinking and start over-trusting is to take our thoughts hostage. This isn't easy. If it was, the verse wouldn't use the word "captive." The word captive means, "a person who has been taken prisoner."

We know our thoughts can run wild and destroy everything in their wake, so we have to lock them up and put them exactly where they belong, focused on Jesus and His loving kindness.

Remember: Anxiety might not be from God, but God allows us to experience emotions like anxiety to remind us of the calmness and stillness we feel when we stop placing so much weight on worry and start worshipping Him to lift the weight of the world.

Replace: Replace your anxiety with peace – a peace that surpasses all understanding.

"And the peace of God, which surpasses all understanding, will guard your hearts and your minds in Christ Jesus." Philippians 4:7

Reflect: What is something you started to overthink today? How can you take your negative thoughts captive and turn them into life-giving thoughts focused on Jesus and all He has already done?

PERFECT Love DRIVES OUT FEAR

Fear

1 John 4:18
*"There is no fear in love, but perfect love casts out fear.
For fear has to do with punishment, and whoever fears
has not been perfected in love."*

Fear comes in so many forms. It can squash our ideas, plant lies in our heads, cause us to worry, and make us doubt God. But that fear, no matter its form, is never from God. Because there is no fear in love and God is love; therefore, there is no fear in God! Fear is just another tactic satan uses to get to us – to really get to us.

Fear shows up when we decide to go for that thing we've always wanted to do, but we are afraid of what people might think or say. Or when we want to take the next step in a job, dream, or relationship, but we're afraid of failure. Fear comes barging in as soon as we find our peace.

If you're like me, you worry about the safety of your loved ones a lot. I have horrible dreams about my husband, my best friends, and my family very often. And that's when I know I'm under a spiritual attack.

Since peace comes from Jesus, the enemy has to find a counter-attack. God moves His chess piece and stills your mind, so satan moves his piece to try to steal your mind. And it might go back and forth for a few minutes, but, spoiler alert: God wins. Which means we win. Which means peace wins over fear. Which means we have the power to choose to be calm in Christ instead of fearful of the "what if."

We are in a world of "what ifs." What if I don't get the job? What if he breaks up with me? What if I don't get into that school? What if they don't like me? What if they were talking bad about me? But we have to know that even if those "what ifs" come true, God is still on the throne. He still wins, and we still win. No scheme of man, or of the enemy, can take that truth away.

My counselor said it best when she said to turn your "what ifs" into "so whats." So what if I fail? So what if they don't like me? So what if I don't get the job? Does God still sit on the throne? Yep. Then, we're good.

Allowing fear to overcome us steals our joy and our time. It steals moments that we can't get back, moments that could grow the Kingdom. Fear makes us think of ourselves more than we think of God. We focus on our weaknesses instead of remembering His strength.

"But he said to me, 'My grace is sufficient for you, for my power is made perfect in weakness.' Therefore I will boast all the more gladly of my weaknesses, so that the power of Christ may rest upon me." 2 Corinthians 12:9

Fear feels weak. Fear makes us overcompensate and start grabbing for whatever we can find to save us from drowning. Fear brings out panic and can pull out the worst in us. But peace. Peace makes us think more sensibly and find safety in a God stronger than our circumstances. Peace helps us float without fear of the future.

We can say no to fear. We don't have to give in. Find refuge in His wings and remember where your fear is coming from. Recall the times when God helped you overcome your fears.

Remember: Fear can teach us how to fight. When the enemy ushers in fear, we see how God ushers courage into our hearts and knocks down any fears we have. Our God has already defeated death, so what else is there for us to fear?

Replace: Replace fear with courage, not just any courage, but courage found in Christ. Courage on your own won't get you nearly as far as the courage you have when you rely solely on Christ.

"Be strong and courageous. Do not fear or be in dread of them, for it is the Lord your God who goes with you." Deuteronomy 31:6

Reflect: What is your biggest fear right now? What is God saying to you about that fear?

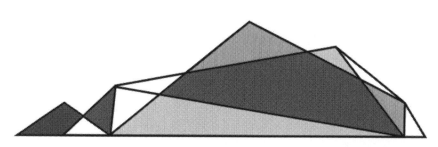

WHEN THE DEVIL FINISHED TEMPTING HIM, HE LEFT HIM UNTIL AN OPPORTUNE TIME

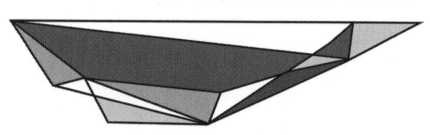

Temptation

Luke 4:13
"And when the devil had ended every temptation, he departed from him until an opportune time."

Just when we think the devil is finished tempting us, he's not. The devil tempted Jesus in the wilderness, and when Jesus didn't give in, he left him. But the last part of the verse says, "until an opportune time." Because he'd be back.

Satan tricks, tempts, and torments, and then lets us think he's given up. But he doesn't give up. He's on the losing side of a spiritual battle, and he's trying to play catch-up. He's going to wait until we are at our weakest, a very opportune time, to pounce again. Satan shows no mercy and gives no grace. He wants to take us down.

While I was writing this, my dad called me and said that he was thinking about one of the first things I ever learned at school. My teacher taught me the phrase, "Just turn and walk away." He said "Kaitlin, you quoted that little mantra repeatedly in the softest little voice." The "stranger danger" phrase and my repetitive whisper etched a memory in my dad's mind that we will laugh about forever. And his anecdote made me think about another stranger in our lives.

The enemy is a stranger. He doesn't know us. We don't have intimacy with him like we do with Jesus. He didn't knit us together in our mothers' wombs. He can't count the hairs on our heads or freckles on our skin. He is not our friend. But he tries to convince us to talk to him and get inside his van to go away with him. The best thing to do is just turn and walk away. Walk away from the temptation he holds out like candy. Walk away from his lies. Walk away from the mistakes of our past he tries to hold over us.

2 Corinthians 4:8 says, "We are afflicted in every way, but not crushed; perplexed, but not driven to despair."

He is going to come at us from every side. He is going to be sneaky. He will try to work in places and through people we least expect. But he will never prevail.

This doesn't mean we won't stumble and fall – it means we won't stay down for long.

If you struggle with sexual sins, satan will try to get you alone with that person you are most attracted to. If you struggle with drinking too much, he will put you in a setting where it seems fine to throw back a few drinks. If you struggle with gossip, he will put you in the breakroom with the co-worker you gossip with the most.

But for every situation the enemy stages, God is there too. When you're alone with that person, God will give you the courage to step back. When you are feeling pressured to push the limits, He will remove your need for approval. When bashing another person starts to make you feel better, He reminds you that everyone is His kid and everyone matters. There is no temptation He can't give you the tools to overcome.

Since Jesus went through temptations just like us, He knows exactly what we need to conquer them all. He equips us with wisdom from His Word to combat anything the enemy tries. We are armed with truth, righteousness, and the Spirit to fight off every attack.

If there are temptations we just can't kick, it would be wise to get in community with people we can talk to, people who can cheer us on and pull us out of the muck. Chances are, they have gone through something similar, and God can use them to guide us. God is all about connection. He makes us better together – together with Him and each other. We were never meant to go it alone. The way He crosses our paths with others is never by accident and always on purpose. He will speak through the people around us and supply us with the words we need to hear to turn the page and step away from what is pinning us down.

Remember: Temptation reminds us there is an enemy on the loose, prowling like a lion and trying his best to kick us when we're down. God reminds us He will never let us be tempted without providing a way out. We can endure and overcome anything with our God.

"No temptation has overtaken you that is not common to man. God is faithful, and he will not let you be tempted beyond your ability, but with the temptation he will also provide the way of escape, that you may be able to endure it." 1 Corinthians 10:13

Replace: Freedom takes the place of temptation. God knows satan uses footholds to try to trap us and torture us, but Jesus came to trample every temptation and toss freedom all over the place like confetti. Now, it's ours for the taking over every single trick the enemy throws at us.

Reflect: What is the one temptation you've been trying to kick? What is one step you can take to start overcoming it today?

a heart at PEACE Gives Life to the body

Comparison

Proverbs 14:30
"A tranquil heart gives life to the flesh, but envy makes the bones rot."

Rotten bones. Yikes! God was not playing around with that one. Being envious of someone else's life will literally rot you from the inside-out.

Comparison and Jealousy are like twin sisters. Comparison tells you to put your life up against someone else's and Jealousy comes along and tells you to envy what they have.

Comparison says your job isn't as cool as hers and Jealousy tells you to pick her apart to make yourself feel better.

Comparison whispers, "Your clothes are not as cute as hers," and Jealousy laughs, "Girlfriend, how will you ever get everything she has?"

It's an endless cycle with these two sisters. They work together to torment you. Their goal is to label you, "Not Enough" so you will be overworked and still underrated.

But that's not what God called you to do. Comparison and Jealousy are not His children.

You see, the enemy wants you to focus on what you lack so that you won't even recognize the abundance God has set before you.

God introduces a couple of His children: Contentment and Joy. He gives you Contentment over Comparison and Joy over Jealousy. He reminds you of who you are in Him and that you are more than enough without being too much.

He never compares us to each other. He never makes us race or fight for His attention or affection. He has the supernatural ability to love us all and listen to us all at the same time. And He wants us to do the same for each other.

Nehemiah had to work with a team to rebuild the walls of Jerusalem. (Read Nehemiah chapters 3 and 4). He could not have done it alone. If he had constantly compared his efforts to the efforts of others, it would have made the process a lot more difficult. We are co-laborers with Christ, building His Kingdom, and if we keep looking at another person's building, we may never finish ours.

It takes a team to do the work of Christ. That's why we are called the **BODY**. A body has many moving parts. You are an important one. Your part is no better or worse than someone else's. All parts are necessary to make the body function as God designed.

"From whom the whole body, joined and held together by every joint with which it is equipped, when each part is working properly, makes the body grow so that it builds itself up in love." Ephesians 4:16

Do you compare your eye to your arm? Of course not! They are incomparable. God uniquely handcrafts each of us; therefore, we are equally incomparable. You are the only person exactly like you on the planet, so don't go around comparing apples to oranges and eyeballs to elbows.

But if you do find yourself slipping back into the comparison trap, try to recall the things which make you different, the things you really like about yourself. Maybe the way your clothes always smell like coffee, or your adorable laugh, or your love for adventure, or the exact way you like your eggs cooked. And when you think about all those little quirks, stop and remember that God loves those things about you, too, because He gave them to you.

It really is time to stop comparing. We talk about it often. We talk about empowering each other and removing jealousy from the game, but we have to do more than talk. Let's move forward lifting each other up; when we do, we are lifted up.

If we are all on the same team, there is never a need to compete. If we are teammates, we do not work against one another. We pass the ball, cheering on our brothers and sisters, and when they score, we know they couldn't have done it without the assist. Let's start acting like the winning team we are!

Remember: Do you remember when comparison started creeping into your life? Maybe it was in middle school or maybe it was when you started dating and sizing yourself up against every other single girl. Now, try to recall times you have felt content with your personality, your appearance, and your purpose. Compare the feelings and free yourself from the constant competition you create with those around you.

"But let each one test his own work, and then his reason to boast will be in himself alone and not in his neighbor." Galatians 6:4

Replace: We have the power in Christ to replace comparison with celebration. It's not easy, but it's necessary if we want to live the life God is offering. When we let God remove the weeds of comparison from the garden of our hearts, we make room for celebration of others to flourish and fill us with the fresh joy that comes straight from God.

Reflect: How many times today did you catch yourself comparing your life to someone you know or someone on social media? Jot down two practical ways you can kick comparison to the curb today.

do not TAKE TO Heart ALL THE THINGS THAT PEOPLE say

Offense

Ecclesiastes 7:21-22
*"Do not take to heart all the things that people say, lest
you hear your servant cursing you. Your heart knows that
many times you yourself have cursed others."*

I had not heard of the "spirit of offense" until two years ago. I also
did not realize I had been walking around with this spirit for most
of my life. Yuck!

I've always chalked it up to being "sensitive," which I definitely
am, but that's no excuse for bitterness and hurt feelings over every
little thing.

Everything is not always about us, and while that may sound
obvious, it's also very hard to remember. We live in a world that
teaches us to focus on ourselves, thus maintaining our emotional,
physical, and spiritual comfort levels. Living this way leads to a
very egocentric life. When we are egocentric, we leave no room for
God or others.

The book, *Free of Me* by Sharon Hodde Miller, talks about turning
our focus inside-out and thinking about Jesus and others before
ourselves, like the old church acronym J-O-Y: Jesus, Others,
Yourself.

I often think negative comments or actions are about me. I get my feelings hurt when someone isn't as friendly to me as I am to them, or when someone doesn't invite me somewhere, or if, God *forbid*, someone unfollows me on social media! Gasp. How could they? What did I ever do to them?

Nothing.

Chances are, all those things I just mentioned have nothing to do with me. That rude co-worker, or that not-so-kind family member, or that friend who isn't really acting like a friend lately? I bet none of that is about us, friends.

When we walk around carrying an offense like a purse, we tend to load it down with every little thing, making it so heavy the strap breaks and everything spills out. It also really hurts your arm when your purse is that heavy, ya know?

I'm not saying some things are not offensive and your feelings can't be hurt. Sometimes people do and say things that really bring pain. While you should extend grace to those who hurt you, it never gives them the green light to continue hurting you.

My mentor shared something with me she read once: "Feel it, then let it pass." So, when you are rightfully offended, don't dwell on it. Feel the pain, acknowledge how it made you feel, then move right along. There is no need for you to sit in the pain – it will not benefit anyone in the world.

In other instances when you over-analyze or take something personally, try to think more about the other person than you do about yourself. They probably never meant to hurt you, and if they did, that's on them and *still* not on you.

Like the verse in Ecclesiastes 7 says, we have done things to cause pain too. Recall the times when you hurt someone, or said something you shouldn't have, or ignored someone because you had a bad day. You probably never meant to wound anyone in any way, and you definitely desired forgiveness for whatever you did.

God tells us not to, "take to heart the things that people say" (Ecclesiastes 7:21). Don't tuck their words away and meditate on them. But do "take heart" because He has overcome the world! (John 16:33)

When we replace offense with gratitude for the people and positive encounters God has given us, we will not remain in a posture of pain, but instead, enter a posture of peace – a peace that really does surpass all understanding and can only be from our Jesus.

Next time your heart starts to feel offense, play some defense. Use God's Word and His promises to defend your heart and your mind from the idea that what someone said or did was meant to take you down – because that feeling is not from Him.

Remember: All of our offenses were removed on the cross — yes, that means the person beside you got made new too. When we feel the weight of forgiveness for how we have sinned against God and others, we simultaneously drop every ounce of offense we have been carrying around.

"And forgive us our debts, as we also have forgiven our debtors." Matthew 6:12

Replace: Get your game face on and sub in grace for offense. Grace is the ultimate game-changer and your ticket to a world where the actions of others neither build you up nor tear you down but remind you to extend the same gift you've been so freely given. When we choose grace over offense, we win every time.

Reflect: Think back to the last time you got seriously offended. What sparked the offense in your heart, and how could you have viewed things differently?

WE ARE

God's

MASTERPIECE

Insecurity

Ephesians 2:10
"For we are his workmanship, created in Christ Jesus for good works, which God prepared beforehand, that we should walk in them."

If we are not fully being ourselves, we cannot fully walk in all God has planned for us. He made you the way you are for a specific purpose. Embracing your divine design is how you take ownership of your God-given purpose.

Bottom line: Insecurity is never from God; insecurity is a liar. Whether someone told you lies or you made them up in your head, they're all pieces of the enemy's puzzle he uses to confuse.

Satan wants you to think there is a piece missing, or you have a piece that's the wrong shape, or there are one too many pieces – all at the same time.

We are told to stop feeling like we are "too much" and "not enough." I've read that phrase in so many books, like the amazing book *Wild and Free* by Jess Connolly and Hayley Morgan, but we put those books down and walk back into our lives, feeling incomplete.

"And you have been filled in Him, who is the head of all rule and authority." Colossians 2:10

We think we're too loud and not pretty enough. We're too fat and not smart enough. We're too silly and not serious enough.

We are called to be imitators of Christ, and the Bible never talks about Him being too much or not enough. Christ is the embodiment of love. He sought and served the outcasts, overlooked and downtrodden. He was so much and more than enough because He risked it all to make sure we wouldn't have to spend eternity without Him.

The idea of insecurity is not new. People have always been insecure because the enemy has always wanted us to feel like we just aren't quite qualified for the work God has assigned. But God never said He'd qualify us with our looks, locations, or vocations. He really never gave us a list of qualifications at all. He just chose us. And He chooses us every day – to be His heart and voice in a world that needs Him so desperately.

The weight of insecurity only holds us back from completing our daily divine assignments. Go ahead and shake the self-doubt off and run with your calling. If you're loud, shout Him from the mountaintop. If you're quiet, whisper for *His* glory.

It doesn't matter what you're like as long as you end up looking like Jesus.

When your security rests on what others think of you, or what you think of you, it will crumble every time. No one can give you the approval God can give you. Imagine yourself and others like puny, inexperienced security guards that are always falling asleep on the job. They let anything and everything in, making it impossible to keep the place secure because they just do not know what they are doing.

But God.

He is the strongest security guard with all the weapons and all the experience anyone could ever need. He ensures what He is guarding is totally safe and 1,000% secure. And guess what else? He never goes off duty. He is always on guard. Now, wouldn't you want to trust in the latter security guard over the former?

God wants to shut out all other voices, including our own, so we hear only His. His still, small voice is what enables us to be more than OK with who He created us to be. Until we become secure in His intricate design and mixture of our personality, hair, skin, eyes, voice, dreams, and gifts, we will keep letting the puny security guard run the show.

Drop the insecurity, and let the strongest guard out there take over for you. You won't regret it.

Remember: *"You shall be a crown of beauty in the hand of the Lord, and a royal diadem in the hand of your God." Isaiah 62:3*

God sees us as a "crown of beauty." Isn't that quite the confidence boost? You don't need a single thing this world has to offer to know you are essential and irreplaceable. Be crowned with His love every day and be reminded royalty comes from Heaven.

Replace: Confidence is the key to cracking the code of insecurity. But our confidence is not found in what we wear, who we hang out with, or where we work – we have a confidence in Christ with a lock that can't be picked with any coat hanger or credit card. Choose to guard your heart with that confidence instead of letting insecurity break in and wreck every room.

"In the fear of the Lord one has strong confidence, and his children will have a refuge." Proverbs 14:26

Reflect: What is your greatest insecurity? Write it down, cross it out, and list all the ways God refutes the lie you have been believing.

For am I now seeking the approval of Man or of God?

People-Pleasing

Galatians 1:10
*"For am I now seeking the approval of man, or of God?
Or am I trying to please man? If I were still trying to
please man, I would not be a servant of Christ."*

I want to chase down every single person who doesn't like me and convince them to love me. But that is not my job. I am doing important Kingdom work, and I cannot pause it all to convince you that my work and my life are important. Kinda like Nehemiah. When the enemies came over to distract him from building the wall, he said, "I cannot come down. I am doing important work." (Read Nehemiah 6 for a story that will fire you up!) Remember, friends: We cannot stop doing what God is calling us to do just to please everyone around us.

The frustrating thing is some of those people I am bargaining with, out of breath from all the chasing, are other Christians. They are people who love the same Jesus I love and are children of the same King as me. We are family. But we don't act like it. We compete and compare and tear each other down. We assume and argue and offend. We act like we aren't even friends, let alone brothers and sisters. How can it be that we've let satan himself slither right into the "big C" Church? When we deny each other, we invite him in.

It was never my cross to bear to convince a single person to like me.

37

And it was never yours either. This doesn't mean we shouldn't love and be kind, but if we are doing those things – if we are loving like Jesus – then the rest is up to Him. We have to leave it in His hands to soften people's hearts toward us.

Sometimes, you just aren't everyone's "cup of tea" (or cup of coffee. I prefer coffee). One of my friend's favorite blog posts is about not being everyone's "Chick-Fil-A sauce." The author talks about how amazed she was to learn that all her friends weren't ordering Chick-Fil-A sauce over Polynesian sauce because it is the *best*. She realized it was the best to her, but not everyone loved it.

Maybe everyone isn't your biggest fan, but that doesn't mean *someone* isn't. And guess what? You totally are the best to Jesus. That sounds cheesy, but it's true. You are His absolute favorite.

Sometimes you just have to take a step back and really think about the people who are cheering you on. Who is fanning your flame?

Make a list if you have to.

My husband and my mom and dad are at the top of my list followed by a powerhouse spiritual mentor and a strong tribe of women. But I know what it is like to feel absolutely alone, like no one is in your corner. The enemy tries his best to isolate us, but we are a royal priesthood (1 Peter 2:9).

When I start listing people who see the best in me, I realize that list is long, and even if there's another list out there with people who aren't all about me, it doesn't matter. If I give all my energy to convincing the other list to move over to the "fan club" list, then I have no energy left to give back to the ones who give me their time, love, and energy. It's not fair to them or me.

In *Free of Me*, Sharon Hodde Miller discusses our need for approval. She said God gave us the need for approval, but wants us to desire it from Him, not people.

But we are flawed, and we look elsewhere for our cups to be filled. We crave attention from peers and strangers on the internet and forget the one Source that can give us all the affirmation we need in an instant. We have to make it a habit to stop the people-pleasing as soon as it comes on and redirect our thoughts to pleasing Him. When we do, the enemy's tactic to distract loses its power. When we try to please Jesus, we are filled up and remember why we are on the planet.

Kindness and people-pleasing are not synonymous. I believe we confuse the two way too often. We think by saying no, not replying, or not attending, we are being rude, when in reality, we are making choices that allow us to best serve Jesus. If we are always saying yes, we are only giving a small part of our hearts to each yes.

God did not intend for us to be spread thin – He wants us to have the room to fully give ourselves to whatever it is we are called to. People-pleasing always leads to being spread thin and worn out. I will be the first to tell you how much I struggle with it. I want everyone to love me and everyone to be happy with what I did for them. But, the people who really love us, and are really for us, don't ever want us to live to please them. They want us to live to please Him, and they will always understand when we have to tell them "no," because they realize we are not doing it to hurt or offend them.

We have to do the same for others. We have to be OK with someone saying "no" because we understand it's not all about us. People-pleasing is a full-circle kind of thing – we don't want anyone to aim to please us either, so treat it like a two-way street.

When we are on the same page about Who we are here to serve, it makes things run much more smoothly. We will stop being scorekeepers because there won't be a scoreboard. Live a life free of the need to please and to be pleased. Be filled up from the One who is bread and water. His well really never runs dry.

We are made for more than words of affirmation from a friend or likes on a photo we posted. All the affirmation you will ever need comes from heart of the God you've been serving.

Remember: Working for multiple masters is way too difficult. Focusing all your attention on pleasing the Master of the Universe will keep you from running in a million different directions in an effort to gain the world. You might disappoint people in the process of finding your calling, but remember that Jesus disappointed people too. Keep your eyes on Jesus, and don't try to go to the ends of the earth to please everyone else.

"The discerning sets his face toward wisdom, but the eyes of a fool are on the ends of the earth." Proverbs 17:24

Replace: Your passion for God takes priority over pleasing everyone. By focusing on exactly what He has asked of you, you remove the pressure you placed on yourself to be everyone's savior. You can serve people and love them well without making it your mission to provide everyone's happiness. Replace the desire to do all the things with the passion to do the things that matter for the One Who matters most.

Reflect: What have you done as a people-pleaser lately? Write down one thing you want to say "no" to but fear you will disappoint someone in the process. Pray over that situation and ask God to guide you on the best way to say "no" so you can make room for the "yes" He has for you.

The Lord will not forsake His people

Loneliness

1 Samuel 12:22
"For the Lord will not forsake his people, for his great name's sake, because it has pleased the Lord to make you a people for himself."

Spending time alone can be very important. God wants us to be alone with Him. But feelings of loneliness and isolation are not from Him. One of the enemy's favorite things is for us to feel like we are walking through life by ourselves, with no one to turn to.

All relationships can be hard. There are seasons when we have a stellar support system and friendships that are the wind beneath our wings. On the flip-side, there are seasons when we wonder if anyone knows we exist.

I've walked through both. How about you?

No one can prepare us for the loneliness we feel in the second season. I have found there are lessons to be learned in every season – whether we can see them at the time or not. While loneliness is not from God, we can still grow in a season of loneliness. He really does work everything together for good (Romans 8:28). I cling to that verse daily because life doesn't always make sense, but God always does, whether we can understand Him or not.

In my season of loneliness, I kept hearing God whisper to me that

He was preparing me to help someone else. When He allows us to experience something, it always gives us the ability to help someone else walking behind us. And if someone is walking behind you, chances are, you are probably walking behind someone else.

Don't sit and wallow in loneliness (as much as you'd love to order takeout for one and lock your door). Reach your hand out and there will be a hand reaching back, ready to pull you out of the pit you're in. Life is a cycle of those who have survived the season and those weathering the storm. We are made to be both kinds of people at various times in our lives.

Start seeing a counselor. Call your mentor. Text a friend. Seek advice from a pastor or a family member. Most importantly, immerse yourself in the Word. The Word of God really does have all the answers you will ever need – you just have to look.

Ups and downs will come. They always do. We will feel lonely one day and have the time of our lives with a group of friends the next. We will experience times of isolation, followed by a calendar full of birthday and wedding invites from loved ones. The key is to reject loneliness and embrace belonging. This does not mean we have to feel like we belong to a "squad" that has the most fun; it means we belong to the greatest Friend there ever was, is, and will be.

And the worst feeling of loneliness we might experience? Church loneliness. It's a thing. It's a thing because satan wants it to be a thing.

Church is where we should feel the least alone, yet, Sunday after Sunday, people walk in looking for community and walk out feeling isolated. Satan will hone in on one thing that did or did not happen and make us think that church is just not the place for us. The truth is, church is always the place for us. We are always welcome. Not because of any of the people in there, but because of the God in there.

I'm certain that in seasons of loneliness, God is there to remind us, "All you need is *Me*." If everyone else on the planet fails us, we still have Him, and He is enough.

1 Samuel 12:22 tells us God never rejects us, and He is *pleased* to make us His own. He delights in spending time with us. When we remember He is first in our lives, other relationships start to fall into place – into their rightful places.

God doesn't have to give us other people to do life with. Everything and everyone, besides Jesus, is extra – but in His goodness and abundance, He chooses to give us community anyway. He wants us to have family, friends and a strong group of believers to walk through struggles and celebrate victories with. Life is just not as much fun when you live it alone.

It's difficult to write this because I've gone through recent seasons of loneliness. It's odd that you can feel so alone in your first year of marriage. The enemy tries to convince you that your marriage isn't good enough. Then, he tries to convince you that your other relationships are suffering because you're putting so much into your marriage. It's a vicious cycle – if you listen to him. You have to push his voice out and hide in the Voice that holds every answer.

In those times when you just want to escape the world and be by yourself, do the opposite. It's not easy, and it goes against your feelings, but that friction will rekindle the fire inside you for community.

Reach out to your friends, to your family, to your church. It may be that no one even knew how you felt, but when you let them know, they will be there to rally around you and remind you how loved you are – by them and by the God of the universe.

Don't do life alone. Find your people. Find your church. Run the race with a team because it's so much better to have people cheering you on.

Remember: God is always with you. You can't ever be alone if God lives in your heart. He also sends people to speak life over you and remind you how loved you are. God loves community and wants you to have it. Loneliness is never part of His plan.

"For where two or three are gathered in my name, there am I among them." Matthew 18:20

Replace: One of the definitions of community is: "a feeling of fellowship with others, as a result of sharing common attitudes, interests, and goals." It's no coincidence that the word unity, meaning "the state of being united or joined as a whole" is a part of community. Loneliness flees when unity with other believers enters the room.

Reflect: Who are the people in your life right now who remind you you're not alone in this world? Write their names down, pray over them, and give them a call today.

Do not worry about your life

Stress

Matthew 6:25
"Therefore I tell you, do not worry about your life, what you will eat or drink; or about your body, what you will wear. Is not life more than food, and the body more than clothes?"

Stress is like a wrecking ball that hits us from all directions – jobs, families, friends, ministries, bills… you name it. We can stress about absolutely everything if we allow our minds to go there.

No matter the type of stress, none of it ever comes from God. He is the Prince of Peace, not the King of Killin' Your Mood. He wants you to experience joy in Him. He tells you not to go around worrying about what you'll eat or drink or wear. In other words, don't sweat the small stuff. Actually, don't sweat anything at all.

Easier said than done, right? Just when I stop stressing over things at work, I start worrying about the safety of my family. When that passes, I get totally freaked out about the future. It is never-ending – until we choose to end it.

I've said it before, and I'll say it again – we have power over our thoughts and minds. A train of thought can only chug along if we allow it. We have the power to derail it. It's time we knock the "Stressed-Out-Soul Train" off its tracks.

I think we sometimes disregard stress as a permanent inhabitant of our minds, but it's really a culmination of thoughts we can learn to control. All stress stems from thinking about something that causes worry, fear, or anxiety – none of which come from God. Then, we start the unhealthy negative thought spiral, sending us to a very low point, gasping for air, for Truth.

And the truth is that not a single hour is added to your life by worrying (Matthew 6:27). So, what's the point?

Our lives are orchestrated by the Author of Creation and Salvation. He wants us to live our lives to the fullest – His fullest. He doesn't want us walking around with tense shoulders and stress-induced hair loss. He knows all about the tensions of life because He was a human. That's why talking to Him when we feel bogged down makes the most sense.

But we don't always turn to Him, do we? Sometimes we turn to shopping, alcohol, sex, popularity, money, or traveling to relieve the stress. But we've been given the one cure for all the tension and all the cares in the world – Jesus. Since stress is not from God, He doesn't want it to consume our lives. He offers solution after solution in the Bible for less stress.

John 14:27 "Peace I leave with you; my peace I give you. I do not give to you as the world gives. Do not let your hearts be troubled and do not be afraid."

Psalm 94:19 "When anxiety was great within me, your consolation brought me joy."

Matthew 11:28 "Come to me, all you who are weary and burdened, and I will give you rest."

He offers peace, joy, and rest in place of what the world offers. When your mind is racing about the troubles you've been facing with your career, take His peace. When your heart is anxious because of a relational problem with a friend or family member, He consoles you with joy. And when your burdens are too heavy to bear, He lifts them off and lets you have some rest.

I would say stress is for the birds, but He said He cares for the birds (Matthew 6:26) and that means He surely cares for us. So, yeah, stress isn't for the birds, and it certainly isn't for you.

Choosing Jesus and choosing contentment, no matter our situation, does not promise a life free of hardships; it does promise that we can avoid stress because we know the end result every single time. His victory is always the end result. There's no situation you could ever experience that doesn't end with victory in Jesus. Boom. Mic drop. No questions. He wins. You win. We win.

Nothing in this world has the power to create a barrier between you and Jesus. That lost job cannot separate you from Him. That breakup cannot separate you from Him. That zit on your wedding day cannot separate you from Him. That betrayal from your closest friend cannot separate you from Him. And the sting of death cannot separate you from Him. So, when you feel stress coming at you from every side, realize where it's coming from and send it right on back. You were made for more than stressing out over every detail of your life. You were made to live free of the chains that drag you down and free from thoughts that bind you up. When you say "yes" to Jesus, you say "no" to sin and stress.

Stress-free is the way to be, right? We have to add and subtract things from our lives on a daily basis in order to balance the equation; so, make it a habit to subtract stress and add Jesus as soon as your feet hit the floor in the morning... even before you check Instagram.

Remember: *"But the fruit of the Spirit is love, joy, peace, patience, kindness, goodness, faithfulness, gentleness, self-control; against such things there is no law." Galatians 5:22-23*

The fruits of the Spirit do not include stress. Stress will not produce any fruit in your life! But peace. Peace will produce delicious fruit that you can see now and later. When your heart is tempted to panic and worry, remember the reward that comes from being at peace with whatever Jesus has planned for you.

Replace: God is peace. When you ask Him to live in your heart forever, then that means peace lives there too. There is no room for stress when peace takes up so much space in your soul. Let God remove every trace of stress and fill you with a type of serenity only found in Him.

Reflect: What are the top three things causing you the most stress right now? Write them down. Then, write beside them how God will work them together for your good and what you can learn from each.

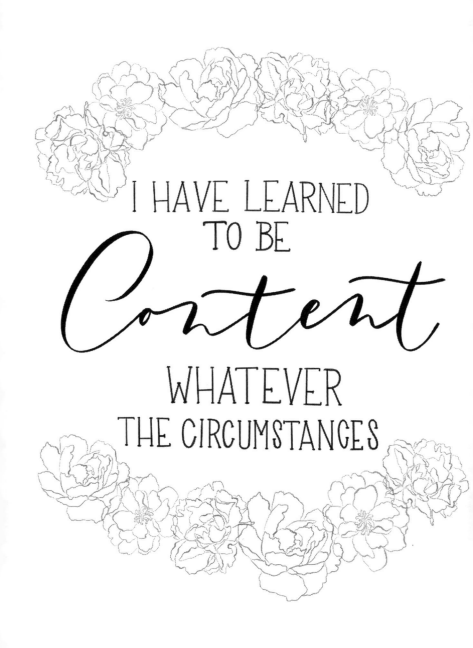

I HAVE LEARNED
TO BE

Content

WHATEVER
THE CIRCUMSTANCES

Discontentment

Philippians 4:11
*"Not that I am speaking of being in need, for I have
learned in whatever situation I am to be content."*

It's no coincidence the day I sat down to write about discontentment, the message I heard at church was about discontentment.

Pastor Mark Pettus from Church of the Highlands said it well when he said we are surrounded by the enemy of contentment. Comparison is on every corner, and we give in more than we fight back. FOMO (Fear Of Missing Out) overwhelms us, and we teleport to anywhere but where we are with the click of a cell phone button.

I never cease to be amazed by Paul's joy and contentment throughout the New Testament. He was in prison praising Jesus. He was shipwrecked, snake-bitten, and stoned, and he still oozed the joy of Christ. You can't fake that kind of joy. He could have easily laid down and cried (like I would probably do in prison), but he just kept going and used his situation as an opportunity to share the gospel. I doubt he was thrilled with what he had, but he was content.

My counselor and I talked about the difference between happiness and joy just the other day. Happiness is always fleeting; if we are always chasing happiness, we will never be content. But joy. Joy can be coupled with sadness or pain or anger or grief or happiness. Joy is constant. Joy overrides all other emotions. Joy and contentment go hand-in-hand.

To be content is to want for nothing and give thanks for everything. When we are content, we aren't looking at her Instagram wishing it was ours or longing for her house. Instead of harboring jealousy, let's say, "I am here where my feet are and I am full of joy because of it."

My husband's favorite saying is: "Be where your feet are." He has to say it to me far too often as my mind wishes my feet were in another person's shoes. He just wants me to see how beautiful my own shoes really are.

When we are in a constant state of comparison with the person beside us or the person on the other side of the screen, we have no time to be grateful. Comparison and gratitude cannot exist in the same space. One is from an evil enemy and one is from a mighty God. And they are at war in our hearts and in our minds. It's not that comparison will never tug on the rope again when we are content; it's that we will yank the rope back over to the gratitude side. Eventually, it will become a gentle sway rather than a forceful jerk. Remember: We have to take our thoughts captive. We have to make positive thinking a habit – and that takes practice.

Contentment is a practice. It's a choice. It's a muscle. It's not natural. Our nature is to err on the side of comparison and jealousy, rather than confidence and celebration. We think the blessings run out and if someone else gets something, there can't possibly be any left for us. On the contrary, the blessings of God never run out, and that is so beautiful and heart-wrecking for sinners like us. There's always enough to go around at God's table. It's like bottomless brunch!

When we start trying to hoard up all the blessings and show the world what we've got just to make sure someone else doesn't seem to have more, things get dangerous. Our hearts turn hard, and we can't receive, or give, the love we were designed to absorb and pour out.

It's an endless cycle really, this discontentment game. We see someone else's money or fame or job or friends. We covet all their things. We wish we had all their things. We wallow in self-pity about how "not-good-enough" we are. And then we start over with someone new. It's not healthy, it's not productive, and it's not Kingdom. We, instead, have to start a new cycle. Wake up. Give God praise for the very breath we breathe. Show gratitude for the ridiculous amount of things we have. Give some of those blessings away to anyone who needs them. And then start over with someone new.

A switch has to flip to turn contentment on, and praise pays the bill to keep it on.

We become the most content when we remember Jesus over and over and over again. Take a step back to the basics. Remember that He died for your sins. Read His Words. Bask in His love. Make it simple. You really are blessed. And I know that's an overused, made-fun-of church word, but it's just so true. The quicker you decide to put on the windbreaker of contentment and shed the heavy coat of discontentment, the quicker you will feel the breeze and stop sweating bullets. It's true. It's real. It's a process, but you can do it.

You can be where your feet are and be joyful about the house you live in, the clothes in your closet, the trips you do get to take, the job you get to work, the area you serve in at church, and the people you get to do it all with. You can. I believe it.

But hey, don't beat yourself up when you have a bad day and go down that winding road of comparison. Just make an effort to stop the car and give yourself enough grace to begin a new route.

Remember: You have a choice: Live with a heart that is always wanting more or live with a heart that cherishes every part of the life you've been given. If you are chasing after God, you already have everything you need.

"... but those who seek the Lord lack no good thing." Psalm 34:10

Replace: It's not hard to figure out that the replacement for discontentment is contentment. It is hard to choose contentment over all the other emotions that lead you to discontentment. Comparison leads to discontentment. Jealousy leads to discontentment. Believing the lie that you aren't good enough leads to discontentment. But filling your day with thankfulness from beginning to end leads to contentment. Confidence in Christ leads to contentment. Happiness for others leads to contentment. Courage to run your own race leads to contentment. You have the power within you to be content – use it.

Reflect: What area of your life do you wish was totally different? Now, list the reasons how that very area can be special to you right now.

Declaration

You are taking back the narrative of your life.

You made it to the end of this book, and you are taking back the narrative of the life God gave you. But this is just the beginning. You have to use these scriptures and truths as a launchpad to propel you forward as you continue shifting your mindset and focusing every thought on Jesus. No one ever said it would be easy, and that's why we're in it together.

God has given you everything and everyone you need to live a life full of purpose and free from the prison satan tries to put you in. You got your get-out-of-jail-free card when Jesus died for you, so start using it, and be bold with it. Don't let anything stop you from remembering every single thing in your life that is from God and using it all to change the world.

And please remember, while many things are not from God in this life, He might still allow them. He has the power to stop anything, but sometimes, He lets us deal with fear or anxiety or comparison to teach us something, to grow us. He always knows what is best for us. In *Tempted and Tried*, Russell D. Moore, dives into James 1:13 – "Let no one say when he is tempted, 'I am being tempted by God,' for God cannot be tempted with evil, and he himself tempts no one." God does not tempt us or taunt us in order to lead us to evil; He tests us to make us complete, lacking nothing, according to James 1:14. He is in the business of refining, not destroying.

Just because He allows us to experience things like stress and discontentment does not mean He devised those plans to take us down. The Light of the world would never do that. He only wants to bring out the good in us. Diamonds are put under pressure and steel is tempered before either reaches its full beauty and potential. When you experience anything that is not from God, remember that He is still with you and will equip you with His power to weather the storm and come out stronger on the other side.

In order to experience a breakthrough, something in you has to break so His glory can come through.

Now, let's get after it. We aren't taking on the victim role any longer. Our story is one of grace and victory. Let's take back our narratives and tell the world of the freedom we've found.

Write down this declaration and put it on your mirror, in your car, at your desk, or all of the above. Say it out loud every day and remind yourself of the direction your life is headed. Your life belongs to the Author of Salvation – don't ever forget it.

I am taking back the narrative of my life today. Feelings I experience that are not from God will no longer have control over me. I am giving my life to Jesus in every way and letting Him write my story like only He can. His Truth will reign in my heart and in my mind. My story is one of victory because it is His story.

Acknowledgments

Thank you.

Thank you to every person who had a hand in helping me birth this book. Writing a book is not a thing one can just do alone – it takes a village.

To my husband: You are my safe place to land and my biggest fan. I'll never be able to express how thankful I am for how you have supported me the past year. You are everything I ever prayed for.

To my parents: Thank you for raising me to know I can do absolutely anything I set my mind to. Mama, you are my hero and my own superwoman. You do it all and look good doing it. I've never had to wonder if you'll be there because you've always been on the front row, yelling for me louder than anyone else. Daddy, I've never met anyone stronger than you. Thank you for giving me that strength. Thank you for showing me what to look for in a husband. Thanks for letting me be Daddy's Girl.

To my brothers: Kristian, you are always my first phone call. I wouldn't make it a single day without you, and I'm so thankful we progressed from bathroom fights to becoming best friends. Keaton, you are the closest thing I have to a twin in this world. I love your desire for knowledge and the way you dream. Reading to you every day when you were little grew my love for words.

To my Gigi: You really always believe in me. You always have. I'm certain I got my love for words from you. And I definitely got my love for coffee from you. This is a step up from Highlights for Kids, don't you think?

To my sister-in-law Sydney: Thank you for editing this book! And thank you for making me laugh with your edits. You are one of the brightest spots of my life.

To my friend Natalia Drumm: You are a rockstar editor and a

champion for women. I am grateful to know you.

To my friend, sister, and mentor Katie Wilson: Thank you for always seeing the best in me. Thank you for writing with me and praying for me. Thank you for taking this Jesus journey right beside me.

To my best friends: You people are saints. I don't know how you put up with me, but you do it really well. Elizabeth, I have no clue how I got through life before I knew you. I never have to worry that I'm alone because I always know I have you. Elise, where do I start? You are my life coach and my favorite after-work phone call. Thank you for cheering so loudly for me. Mary Alan, you know my soul. Thank you for loving me through the darkest and brightest days. Thank you for seeing the rainbow when I couldn't. Kekoria Greer, I don't know a better person than you and I can't believe I get to call you my friend and sister. Thank you for making me better and loving me so well. Jeri, you're my person. Not many people can say they've been friends for 26 years, and I'm thankful I get to say that with you. You just get me. And you love me unconditionally.

To Leslie: Your artwork made this book what it is. Your talents blow me away, and I am so grateful for our friendship and our collaboration. Let's go cry at P.F. Chang's again very soon.

To my Church of the Highlands family: Thank you for being a house that breeds excellence. I have learned so much about Jesus from all of you because you are truly His hands and feet.

To Amy Seiffert and Toya Poplar: Thank you for the edits, the encouragement, and the friendship. You both shine brighter than the sun.

To Emily Beckham: Thank you for dealing with me and for printing the first ever rough, rough copy of this book. You are an angel.

To every single person who will read this book: You matter. You are loved. You are the reason I write. God sees you and hears you and loves every part of you. Don't listen to the lies that are not from Him. Hide in the truths that come straight from God and give Him the narrative of your life.

To anyone struggling with depression: Do not do it alone. Reach out to someone. Reach out to me. This world will not be as beautiful without you, so please don't listen to a single thought that says it will be. That is not from God.

To my Jesus: Thank You for making me wait on Your timing for this book. Thank You for loving me, all of me. I promise to follow You with my whole heart, my whole life. You amaze me every single day. I can't thank You enough for giving me words to write for others to read for Your glory.

Notes

Chapter 1: Anxiety

1. Senior Pastor of Elevation Church, "When Anxiety Attacks" sermon, Oct. 2016, https://elevationchurch.org/sermons/when-anxiety-attacks/

Chapter 5: Offense

1. Sharon Hodde Miller, *Free of Me: Why Life Is Better When It's Not About You* (Baker Books, 2017)

Chapter 10: Discontentment

1. Pastor Mark Pettus, Church of the Highlands, "The Secret of Contentment," sermon, April 2018, https://www.churchofthehighlands.com/media/message/the-secret-of-contentment

Declaration

1. Russell D. Moore, Tempted and Tried: Temptations and the Triumph of Christ (Crossway, 2011)

Connect with Kaitlin!

Visit kaitlinchappellrogers.com to read more from Kaitlin and book her to speak at your next event!

📷 @kaitlinchappellrogers

f @kaitlinchappellrogers

🐦 @kchaprogers

Made in the USA
Columbia, SC
15 August 2019